THE BIG GULP

The Adventures of a Reluctant Missionary

A creative study of the book of Jonah

THE BIG GULP

The Adventures of a Reluctant Missionary

A creative study of the book of Jonah

BY RICK BUNDSCHUH

ILLUSTRATED BY SCOTT ANGLE

Standard Publishing
Cincinnati, Ohio

TABLE OF CONTENTS

Cover illustration by Scott Angle
Cover design by Dina Sorn
Edited by Tom Finley and Dale Reeves

**Library of Congress Cataloging-in-
Publication Data:**

Bundschuh, Rick, 1951-
    The big gulp : the adventures of a
reluctant missionary : a creative
study of the book of Jonah / by Rick
Bundschuh; illustrated by Scott Angle.
        p.   cm.
    ISBN 0-7847-0736-7
    1. Bible. O.T. Jonah--Study and
teaching 2. Church work with
teenagers. I. Title.
    BS1605.5.B86 1997
    224'.9206--dc21   97-33175
                                    CIP

The Standard Publishing Company,
Cincinnati, Ohio.
A Division of Standex International
Corporation.

04   03   02   01   00   99   98   97

5   4   3   2   1

HOW TO USE THIS BOOK

At first glance the book of Jonah seems to be a short biography about a particularly stubborn man. But Jonah is much more than that. The book of Jonah is really about each of us. It is about God's love for us and his will for our lives. It's about the futility of trying to wiggle out of doing what God wants us to do.

It is a book about God's absolute power over nature and man. Yet it shows how God has intentionally limited himself to use men and women to communicate his concern, displeasure and loving forgiveness to all.

Jonah is really a glance in the mirror. It reflects our self-willed nature. While the story is drawn in large and colorful pictures—destruction of cities, storms at sea and man-eating fish—it still accurately reflects how we often react to God in small ways. We avoid thinking about God; when we think about him, we pull the covers over our heads and hope he leaves us alone.

Most of all, Jonah is about redemption. God's care and love for all people is so great that he will make sure that even a motley crew like the citizens of Nineveh get a chance to hear about his offer of salvation. Good thing for them. And a good thing for us!

Each lesson plan in this book is divided into three sections: **Waxing Up, Taking Off** and **Fully Barreled.** Why the surfing terms? Jonah spent a lot of time riding the waves, that's why! Surfers wax up their boards before they go in the water—the wax makes the board less slippery. They take off on a wave, and, if they can get to the perfect spot on a tubular wave, they are "barreled." Each of these sections presents more than one option for you to choose as learning activities. These are represented by the ♛ icon.

Begin your meeting by involving your students in one or two of the suggested **Waxing Up** activities. These fun options should help you grab attention so that students are focused and ready to learn. Introduce the topic of the lesson in this way.

The **Taking Off** section gives your kids opportunity to innovatively explore the book of Jonah. As in the other sections, there are two recommended activities from which to choose. You may elect to do one or more of these activities, depending on your time limit and the personality of your group.

In each **Fully Barreled** section, you'll find closing activities to help your gang apply the truths they've studied to their own lives. Again, select and use the closing that's most appropriate for your group.

Every activity that requires items you must provide has a "materials needed" sidebar. Please note that all lessons require paper, pens or pencils and Bibles for each student. Because you must always supply these, they are not normally mentioned in the materials lists. Be sure to check your classroom now for these items.

Each lesson plan features two reproducible student activity sheets. The sheets are found at the end of each lesson plan. Slap them on your copy machine and give them to your kids as instructed in each lesson. Make sure you make enough for any unexpected visitors.

Scattered throughout each lesson are the "Check This . . ." sidebars. Some feature extra information for you, others offer optional activities to help fill a longer class time. Some list Christian songs—it's always a good idea to have some contemporary Christian music playing as your students enter the room or as a point of discussion during the lesson.

Finally, take a look at the "Bonus Event," which is really an optional outreach event. Set up as an indoor or outdoor beach party, this event is designed to bring young people into contact with Jesus. It's a beach party done either in the summer or dead of winter complete with movies, music and an outreach message. Your kids will love it and will bring their friends. Jonah would approve!

May God bless you and your teenagers as you get on board *The Big Gulp!*

THE BIG GULP

CLIP ART PROMO PAGE

THE BIG GULP

YOU GOTTA BE KIDDING, GOD!

Lesson Text
Jonah 1:1-3; Matthew 5:44; 19:19; Luke 6:27-36

Lesson Focus
God may call on us to do things that seem hard or impossible.

Lesson Goals
As a result of participating in this lesson, students will:
• Be able to explain why Jonah wanted to avoid Nineveh.
• Give examples of tough assignments God gives Christians.
• Create a plan to carry out a tough assignment this week.

God asks a lot of us.

The prophet Jonah certainly thought so. His job was to spread God's message of repentance and forgiveness, but when he was ordered to preach to the hated people of Nineveh, Jonah turned tail and ran.

Jonah had been sent to perhaps the meanest, deadliest, most wicked spot on the planet. It was the nest of the Assyrians, Israel's sworn enemies. Jonah feared for his neck.

If you have ever had a genuine enemy, you might understand how Jonah felt. God calls you to love that enemy—not tolerate—love! To do good for him. To not speak evil of him. To pray for him. To want and work for his salvation.

God asks tough things of us, there is no doubt.

In the busy social world of high school, there are plenty of opportunities to end up on someone's enemy list. Just to be a little prettier, smarter or more talented than the next person can make you someone's hated rival! But as Christians we also are to do what God commands. His message today varies little from the one he gave Jonah.

This lesson will encourage your students to do what God commands without fear.

 WAXING UP

♛ THE LAST PLACE ON EARTH

This activity is designed to stir up the same feelings that Jonah might have had when God told him to preach to the hated and feared people of Nineveh.

Give each student a copy of "The Last Place on Earth" student sheet. Read the instructions aloud, then allow a few minutes for everyone to work individually on the assignment.

Materials needed:
Reproducible student sheet on page 13 of this book; writing utensils

Check This . . .
   The imaginary communities listed on the reproducible student sheet for this assignment aren't so imaginary. For example, "Stabyoorbackia" is really a South American tribe that glorifies treachery.

Materials needed:
Small slips of paper; pencils

Check This . . .
   Play the song "Harder Than It Seems," by the band Guardian, from their *Bottle Rocket* CD. Discuss why following God is sometimes harder than it seems.

Materials needed:
Reproducible student sheet on page 15 of this book; writing utensils; Bibles

When almost everyone is finished, start a discussion by asking the following questions:
   • **Which places did you least want to visit?**
   • **Why did you feel that way?**
   • **Did you have time to come up with your own terrible place?**

After students have shared their responses, conclude by saying, **"Today we are going to take a look at someone who was told by God to go to the worst place on the planet. We'll see what sort of reaction he had to the idea."**

Move on to your next chosen activity.

♕ ♕ WITNESS THIS

Tell your students that, instead of staying inside for today's lesson, you are taking them to a particularly unseemly area of your town to share Christ on the street corners. Make a big deal about the extreme importance of sharing the gospel even in the face of the difficult nature of doing cold street evangelism in this area.

Say, **"To be absolutely sure that your hearts are really in this, so that our time of spreading the good news will be effective, let's have a secret vote to decide whether we should go there or stay here. The majority will rule."**

Distribute slips of paper and pencils, then allow students to vote. Your group will very likely vote by a wide majority to just stay put. Whichever way the vote goes, explain, **"To be honest with you, I had no intention of taking you out street witnessing today. Instead, I wanted you to sense the kind of apprehension that the guy in today's Bible study felt when he was told by God to do something very similar. Let's take a closer look at Jonah."**

◆ TAKING OFF

♕ NOTE ABOUT NINEVEH

Form pairs, and have partners work on the "Note About Nineveh" reproducible student sheet together. Have them follow along as you read aloud the information about the city, or have a volunteer read the material.

Assemble students into small groups of 4-5 and have them read Jonah 1:1-3. Help those who may not be familiar with the minor prophets locate the book in the Bible. Then let them complete the "Marching Orders" section of the student sheet.

Tell everyone, **"We can imagine that Jonah had both**

fear and revulsion at the thought of being a missionary to the folks of Nineveh. Many of us in the same situation would have run away too!"

Direct your students to the "Tough Assignments" section of the reproducible. Comment, **"Please detail on your worksheet what you have been told by Christ to do and then select one of those assignments to demonstrate as a short play or pantomime in a modern-day setting."**

Select one or more groups to present their skits. When everyone is done, ask questions such as these:

• **At your school, what are some things that tend to make students enemies with one another?**

• **Without naming names, can you think of people you know who are enemies with each other? If so, how would you feel if God told you to go make peace between the very worst of those enemies?**

• **What would you do?**

• **What might Jesus have done, based on what he said in the Scriptures you just read?**

Check This . . .
Racism is a major problem at many schools. This activity gives you a chance to talk about racism and the response Christ would have to it.

♛ ♛ JONAH'S DIARY

Have students read Jonah 1:1-3. In small groups, have them create a journal or diary entry that expresses Jonah's thoughts and feelings about going to Nineveh.

When ready, let volunteers read from their diaries. Discuss the following questions:

• **Why might Jonah have been reluctant to follow God's command?**

• **Does Jonah's response mean he was unspiritual?**

• **How should we act when similar thoughts or feelings come upon us?**

• **How would you feel if God told you to go make peace between the very worst of enemies at your school?**

• **What would you do?**

• **What might Jesus have done, based on what he said in the Scriptures you just read?**

Materials needed:
Bibles; blank paper; writing utensils

3 FULLY BARRELED

♛ MY FAVORITE ENEMY

Distribute slips of paper or index cards to everyone in the class. Say to your group, **"I would like each one of you to privately and personally consider one person whom you have no particular interest in nor warm feelings toward—a person who needs God's love to shine**

Materials needed:
Index cards or slips of paper; writing utensils

through you to them. Please write his or her name or initials on the card. Turn the card over and write one thing that you might be able to do to move toward them this week."

Do not ask anyone to share this information. Close in prayer.

♛ ♛ LOVE IN ACTION

With your students, plan an opportunity to minister to the homeless at a rescue mission, take severely handicapped children out to an event, or work in a nursing home. Challenge your kids to stretch their boundaries and to move toward those who seem to be unlovely or unlovable.

After setting the time and date, be sure to mail or phone a reminder to the students before the day of your activity.

Materials needed:
Anything necessary for chosen service project

The Last Place ON EARTH

Take a look at some of the imaginary places below. Now imagine this: You are in sales; it's your job to sell "Hot Marmies" (whatever they are) to the people in one of these communities. Which is the place you would least like to go? Why?

Gourmet City

A community where cannibalism is accepted and normal. Where strangers are eyed with the wonder of how they might go with onion sauce. A place where everyone seems hungry.

Stabyoorbackia

A community of traitors. A place where people actually delight in drawing you in, only to betray you, steal from you and suddenly do you in. In fact, they live to see the expression on your face when you finally realize that everyone was just pretending to like you.

Happy Island

A place where they sacrifice children to appease their gods, a ritual they do not think is wrong or have any remorse over. These sacrifices are public spectacles and done regularly.

A Really Bad Public School

A community made up of extremely violent people. You could be killed or maimed at a moment's notice for no particular reason other than someone was having a bad hair day. You must be armed and alert at all times.

Can You Do Us One Better?

We have thought of some pretty lousy places to go work. Perhaps you can think of one even worse. Write your idea here. Make it terrible without making it obscene or too gross.

Note About NINEVEH

Nineveh was the capital city of a bunch of rough and tough folks called the Assyrians. This warring nation gave big lickings to Israel. Here's a fast look at the Assyrians and Nineveh.

ASSYRIANS:
- Anti-God
- Looted many other nations
- Had a nasty habit of skinning guys alive
- Piled enemies' skulls in the town squares of the conquered

NINEVEH:
- A hotbed of prostitution (pun intended)
- A center for witchcraft
- Nineveh was so bad that God himself said it "stunk to high heaven" (a fairly accurate paraphrase).

MARCHING ORDERS
Read Jonah 1:1-3 and fill in the blanks with the correct information.

The _____ of _____ came to Jonah. He was told to _____ against the _____ city of _____ . He was told to do this because of the city's _____ . But Jonah _____ from _____ and headed for the distant city of _____ . Starting his journey at the port of _____ , he found a ship headed for _____ . His reason for getting on board was to _____ from God.

TOUGH ASSIGNMENTS
God sometimes gives us hard assignments we would rather run from. Read the following Scriptures and write out the various assignments that you have been given:

Luke 6:27-36
You are assigned by Jesus to:

Matthew 5:44
You are assigned by Jesus to:

Matthew 19:19
You are assigned by Jesus to:

THE RUNAWAY

Lesson Text
Jonah 1:1-16

Lesson Focus
Running from our Christian responsibilities means trouble.

Lesson Goals
As a result of participating in this lesson, students will:
• Learn more about Jonah's runaway attempt.
• Describe ways that Christians run from responsibility.
• Discuss what can happen to others when a Christian ducks his or her duty.
• Examine ways they might be trying to duck God's will.

Run and hide! That's what our sinful nature wants to do when God starts making demands.

From Adam and Eve ducking in the bushes to contemporary men and women on a psychiatrist's couch shifting blame, we all dodge for cover when brought face to face with our sin.

Christian teens who find they have compromised their faith often take the Jonah route. They turn and go fast and furiously away from God. It was futile in Jonah's day and it's futile now.

Today's look at Jonah focuses on his sojourn in the belly of a fish. Three important lessons will be examined: We need to own up to our responsibilities; others can be hurt when we run from God; God demonstrates love by hounding us until we return to him.

◆ 1 WAXING UP

♛ THE FUGITIVE

Use this little story to help your students imagine themselves in the same line of business as Jonah—a fugitive. Read the story, then have students work in pairs to answer the discussion questions. Allow a few minutes for class discussion.

"Walking home from school one day, you happen to stumble upon a briefcase. Opening it, to your astonishment you find a million dollars and a note that reads, 'Dear Pinky, here is the money that I got shaking down the local drug dealers. Hope the boss is happy.' The note is signed by somebody named Blackjack.

It's Mafia money! You decide then and there to do good with the cash, so off you run to a children's relief

> **Check This . . .**
> Play the song "Strangers in the House of the Lord," by **Three Crosses,** from their release **Jefferson Street.**

agency. They get all excited, shake your hand, call you a hero and take your money to feed children in famine areas across the world.

Unfortunately, word soon gets back to the Mafia about all this. Needless to say, they are not pleased. They decide to permit you to view the bottom of the nearest river in a pair of their finest concrete boots. You know you have to get out of town."

Describe what you would do to get away from the evil hand of these gangsters:

- **How would you live?**
- **Where would you go?**
- **What habits would you change?**

♔ ♔ THE CHASE

Before class, locate a great movie car chase scene (try "Bullitt" or "The Rock"). Even better are chase scenes shot from a helicopter. The TV show "COPS" has a whole video shot from this vantage point.

Introduce your video clip by saying something like this: **"In the movies, a great chase scene is often the high point of the film. Let's watch an example of a great chase and then talk about what we would do in that situation."**

Show the clip, then to shift your students' brains into gear, use the following discussion questions after the showing:

- **If, in real life, you were the one being pursued as in this film, would you have given up before being caught or killed?**
- **Do you think you could have escaped your pursuer?**
- **What if you were being chased by a helicopter with heat-seeking capabilities?**
- **Why do you think people run even when they know they have no way to escape?**

Move on to the next step in the lesson by saying, **"We have seen an example of a great chase. Today we are going to take a look at another attempt to escape— one that was pointless from the beginning."**

◆ 2 TAKING OFF

♔ GOING OVERBOARD

Assemble students into small groups of 4-6. Read Jonah 1:1-16 aloud, then assign each group one or more of the following activities:

Materials needed:
VCR and monitor; videotape of a car chase scene

Materials needed:
Blank paper; writing utensils; a video camera;
blank videotape; VCR and monitor

• Write a letter from the captain of the ship to the owners of the cargo that was tossed overboard. Explain what happened and why their stuff is in Davy Jones' locker.

• Use a video camera to create a tabloid TV show that features the events spoken of in the text as well as imaginative interviews with the passengers on the ship. If no camera is available, perform this as a skit.

• Imagine that you are one of the people on the boat with Jonah. Since you think you are going to die at sea, write down your last will and testament as if it were going to be slipped into a bottle and tossed overboard.

When the groups have completed their work, allow them to share with the rest of the students. Ask questions like these:

• **Why do you think Jonah ran?**

• **Do you think Jonah really thought he could hide from God? If not, what do you suppose he expected to happen to him for his disobedience?**

• **Who were some of the people who stood to be hurt because of Jonah's sin?**

• **Can other people be hurt when a Christian runs from God? Give some examples.**

Continue with the next activity or move on to **Fully Barreled.**

♔ ♔ Who Suffered?

Ask your students to work on the "Who Suffered?" student sheet. When they are done working, discuss these questions:

• **Can a person successfully run from God? If not, why would a person attempt to do so?**

• **Do you think God chases everyone? Why or why not?**

• **How does God pursue people? Share some examples.**

• **Does God ever chase you? How?**

3 Fully Barreled

♔ The Moral of the Story

Distribute poster paper and felt-tip markers to each student. Comment, **"I want you to think about the lesson and realities that we have witnessed in the life of Jonah and then write a moral to the story up to this point. It can be in the form of a poem or snappy saying. Just make sure that you have clearly stated what you feel is the moral or lesson for all of us."**

Materials needed:
Reproducible student sheet on page 21 of this book; Bibles; writing utensils

Materials needed:
Poster paper; a variety of colored felt-tip markers

When students have finished, ask them to read what they have written to the rest of the group. Have them take their morals home and post them where they can be reminded not to try to run from God.

♛ ♛ AM I A RUNNER?

Materials needed:
Reproducible student sheet on page 23 of this book; writing utensils

Ahead of time, make copies of the reproducible student sheet on page 23 of this book. Distribute copies of the sheet, then ask students to prayerfully complete it. Let them know that you won't be looking at their answers.

Invite them to complete the two sentences at the bottom:
• **I feel like I've been running from you by . . .**
• **Please help me to deal with this the way you'd like me to. One thing I could do with your help is . . .**

Close your time together by asking them to pray these sentences silently.

WHO SUFFERED?

Read Jonah 1:1-16. Describe how each of the following people suffered from Jonah's decision to run away from God.

THE CAPTAIN OF THE BOAT:

THE CREW:

THE MERCHANTS WHO SENT GOODS ON BOARD:

THE OTHER PASSENGERS:

JONAH:

Now Try This:

When Christians disobey God, other people can be hurt. The following situations describe people who are not being obedient to some of God's commands. Tell who else suffers and in what ways they might suffer.

A CHRISTIAN KID WHO IS AFRAID TO TALK ABOUT HIS FAITH:

A WOMAN WHO LEAVES HER HUSBAND AND CHILDREN TO RUN OFF WITH ANOTHER MAN:

A CHRISTIAN WHO PARTIES HARD ON THE WEEKENDS BUT ACTS HOLY IN CHURCH ON SUNDAYS:

A GUY WHO CONVINCES HIS GIRLFRIEND THAT IF SHE REALLY LOVED HIM SHE WOULD HAVE SEX WITH HIM:

A CHRISTIAN KID WHO NEVER CHIPS HIS OR HER FAIR SHARE INTO THE CHURCH OFFERING PLATE:

Am I a Runner?

Circle the number that best describes you in each of the situations below.
Be honest. This is not a test. No one will ask for your answers.

When it comes to telling others about my faith in Christ . . .

I'm a Runner   **I Do What God Asks**
1   2   3   4   5   6   7   8   9   10

When it comes to being morally pure . . .

I'm a Runner   **I Do What God Asks**
1   2   3   4   5   6   7   8   9   10

When it comes to loving those who are unlovely . . .

I'm a Runner   **I Do What God Asks**
1   2   3   4   5   6   7   8   9   10

When it comes to acting like a Christian at home . . .

I'm a Runner   **I Do What God Asks**
1   2   3   4   5   6   7   8   9   10

When it comes to being honest and not cheating . . .

I'm a Runner   **I Do What God Asks**
1   2   3   4   5   6   7   8   9   10

When it comes to being a giver with my actions, time and money . . .

I'm a Runner   **I Do What God Asks**
1   2   3   4   5   6   7   8   9   10

Dear Lord:
I feel like I've been running from you by . . .

Please help me to deal with this the way you'd like me to. One thing I could do with your
help is . . .

CONSEQUENCES

Lesson Text

Jonah 1:1-17; Matthew 18:15; 1 Corinthians 5:11; 2 Thessalonians 3:14

Lesson Focus

All actions have consequences. Wise choices make for positive consequences; bad choices bring on rotten results!

Lesson Goals

As a result of participating in this lesson, students will:

• Learn the consequences suffered by Jonah for his disobedience.

• Describe the relationship between particular actions and consequences.

• Discuss how to help a person caught up in actions that produce bad results.

• Become accountable to each other to help guard against foolish actions.

Consequences happen.

Put nitro and glycerin together for a little shaking and the consequences are explosive. Violate God's spiritual laws and suffer the spiritual and physical consequences.

Example? Jonah. Run from God and you may find yourself rubbing against the belly of a fish—from the inside.

An object lesson for all believers, Jonah earned a bucketful of consequences for his disobedience. He miserably hunkered down in the hold of a ship as a storm of consequences tossed it about like so much flotsam. Jonah stoically faced the prospect of death at sea but was not prepared for the surprise that God had readied for him. God still had lessons for Jonah to learn. They would be taught the hard way—in the belly of the fish.

Young people can feel that somehow the fruits of their actions will never ripen. They seem to think that they will be the exception to the rule, the lucky one, the one with the ability to dodge disaster. But as the old adage says, "There are no exceptions to God's law—only illustrations of it."

Because not all consequences are immediate, the real relationship between deeds—good or bad—and their results, is sometimes not clear to young people. As your students explore the sure and effective consequences that resulted from Jonah's disobedience, they will gather wisdom about actions and consequences.

Check This . . .
As students are arriving, play the song or show the video "The Hardway," by dc Talk, from their album Free at Last.

◆1 WAXING UP

♛ DID I SAY THAT?

Distribute copies of the reproducible student sheet on page 29 of this book. This page features foolish or shortsighted comments made by real people. Go over the

Materials needed:

Reproducible student sheet on page 29 of this book

comments one at a time as a class discussion, having students describe what was said and the consequences of the mistakes made. You can also have a vote to see who the students think were the silliest or most foolish people.

Conclude this activity by saying, **"As these examples demonstrate, there is a cost for the blunders we commit, even if we think we are right at the time. Today we are going to take a look at the consequences that Jonah was forced to face for doing his own thing."**

Continue with the next activity or move on to **Taking Off.**

♛ ♛ QUESTIONS AND CONSEQUENCES

This is an activity of questions and consequences. You ask the questions, and your students face different consequences depending on their answers.

Here is how to do it: Write your questions on index cards (see the examples below or create your own), one question per card. Place the cards in a stack. Make two more stacks of cards, one stack being silly consequences for students who give wrong answers and the other rewards for students who answer correctly. Use the positive and negative consequences suggested below or think up some of your own. Sample questions:

• **Which author (other than God, the author of the Bible) has his books translated into more languages than any other person?** *(Answer: Lenin)*

• **What is the name of Dorothy's dog in** *The Wizard of Oz?* *(Answer: Toto)*

• **Who is the founder of Microsoft, the computer software giant?** *(Answer: Bill Gates)*

• **What kind of shark is the deadliest in the world?** *(Answer: The great white)*

• **Videocassettes were originally sold in two formats—VHS and what else?** *(Answer: Beta)*

Sample consequences for a wrong answer:

• **Run around the room acting like a chicken**
• **Smell three different armpits**
• **Hold your toes and walk around the room**
• **Sing "Mary Had a Little Lamb"**
• **Do an Elvis impersonation**

Sample consequences for a right answer:

• **A dollar bill**
• **A cold soda**
• **A back rub**
• **A candy bar**
• **An exemption from playing this dumb game again**

Explain to your students, **"Today we are going to take another look at Jonah. As you know if you've been** with us lately, Jonah tried to get far away from God to avoid doing what God had commanded. This time we'll look at one of the strangest incidents in the entire Bible. It's the story of the consequence Jonah faced for his decision to run from the Lord."

2 TAKING OFF

♕ THE STORM

Hand out paper, pencils and Bibles. Have your students follow along as you read Jonah 1:1-17. Say, **"Get together in pairs to go over these verses again. On your paper, list all of the consequences you can find for Jonah's disobedience."**

Students should come up with most of the following:
• *God sent a storm.*
• *The ship was in danger of breaking up.*
• *The people on the ship were in a panic.*
• *The cargo was tossed overboard and lost.*
• *Jonah was thrown overboard as a sacrifice.*
• *The sailors made vows to God.*
• *Jonah was gulped down by a fish.*

Ask your students, **"Can you find anything good that came from this whole incident at sea?"**

The sailors saw God's hand in the storm and put their trust in him. Jonah was being an unknowing evangelist even as he was trying to hide from God.

♕ ♕ CAUSE AND EFFECT

Give each student paper and a pencil. Direct half of your students to describe (in written form) situations that would likely lead to bad consequences. (For example: stealing, lying, cheating or smoking.) The other students are to describe situations likely to lead to good consequences.

When ready, collect the papers and switch them so that the students who wrote about the bad situations trade with students who described the good situations. Hand out new pieces of paper and tell everyone to create another consequence that might occur for the situation they have been given.

Let the students talk about their work. Ask them to name several sins that are common problems for people their age (list these on the chalkboard). Lead a class discussion based on one or more of the sins you've listed by using the following questions:

• **What are some consequences that can happen to a Christian who commits this sin?**

Materials needed:
Bibles; paper; writing utensils

Check This . . .
Play the song "Flames of Truth," by Sarah Masen, from her self-titled debut release. Discuss the consequences of trying to avoid God's truth in our lives.

Materials needed:
Blank paper; writing utensils; chalkboard and chalk

Check This . . .
Ask your students to create a drama, pantomime, video or even paper-bag puppet show which puts Jonah's story in a modern context. For example, a Christian with a hidden sin brings his problems to an entire youth group. Then go over the questions about sin in the text.

• What could happen to his or her family or friends?

• What could happen in his or her church or youth group?

• Is a church better with or without people who commit this sin? Why or why not?

• Why do you think people who know that wrong actions can have severe consequences still choose to sin?

 ## 3 FULLY BARRELED

♛ HOW TOUGH DOES IT NEED TO BE FOR **YOU?**

Distribute copies of the student sheet on page 31 of this book. Let students share their responses with a neighbor, then tell them to prayerfully consider how they respond to the consequences that come their way when they are disobedient.

♛ ♛ ACTION PLAN

Have students work on the "Action plan" section of the student sheet. Be sure they get together in pairs to form a plan for accountability.

Close by asking God to provide encouragement for your students to do those things that bring about good consequences.

Materials needed:
Reproducible student sheet on page 31 of this book; writing utensils

Materials needed:
Reproducible student sheet on page 31 of this book; writing utensils

Check This . . .

For years the story of Jonah has taken a licking by those hoping to show that the Bible is a myth. The idea of a fish gulping down a man who eventually survives seems preposterous.

Yet, fully documented incidents in modern times exist. Fishermen, swallowed whole by sharks, have been rescued alive in this century.

We know that God has designed sharks and other fish plenty big enough for Jonah to fit inside. It is well within God's power to put such a creature in the right place at the right time with a powerful appetite!

DID I SAY THAT?

Sometimes people get it wrong. They underestimate, they overestimate, they think too much of their own abilities, too little of the abilities of another or they simply see themselves as invincible. Each of the people below got it wrong in their own unique way. Be prepared to tell how and what the consequences were.

"I could whip all the Indians on the continent with the Seventh Cavalry."
—*General George Armstrong Custer*

"I cannot imagine any condition which would cause the ship to founder. I cannot conceive of any vital disaster happening to this vessel. Modern ship-building has gone beyond that."
—*E.J. Smith, captain of the* Titanic

"Come, come! Why they couldn't hit an elephant at this dist . . ."
—*Major General John Sedgwick, shot dead while looking over a bunker at the Confederate forces on the other side of the battlefield*

"No Civil War picture ever made a nickel."
—*Irving Thalberg, head of MGM production, as he turned down rights to Margaret Mitchell's book,* Gone With the Wind

"Nothing has come along that can beat the horse and buggy."
—*Advice from businessman Chauncey Depew to his nephew who wanted to invest $5,000 with a wide-eyed ex-bicycle repairman by the name of Henry Ford*

How Tough Does It Need to Be for YOU?

Some people insist on learning lessons the hard way. Look at the descriptions below and circle the phrase where you usually wind up *before* you turn around and obey God.

Hearing God hollering at me

Getting on the boat going in the wrong direction

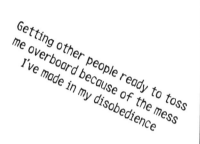
Getting other people ready to toss me overboard because of the mess I've made in my disobedience

Finding myself going the opposite way from where God wants

Starting to get tossed around by the circumstances I've created

Trying to hide away from the influence of God

Getting completely swallowed up by trouble

Action plan

"There's right and there's wrong. Ya gotta do one or the other."
—John Wayne, in *The Alamo*

Make a workable plan for actions and attitudes that are sure to have good consequences. Write out your plan and share it with a friend who will keep you accountable by checking this week to see if you've made an honest attempt to keep your commitment.

actions

attitudes

REPENT!

Lesson Text
Jonah 2:1–3:10

Lesson Focus
Turning from wrong can become a habit.

Lesson Goals
As a result of participating in this lesson, students will:
• Be able to explain what repentance really means.
• Describe how Jonah demonstrated repentance.
• Discuss the signs that accompany genuine repentance.
• Have the option to create a special prayer meeting to pray for a godly turnaround in a specific area.

Few people take the word "repentance" seriously these days. Perhaps we have seen one too many cartoons of the robed zealot walking down the street with "repent" sign held aloft. The word seems to have an archaic ring to it—it just doesn't fit our worldly modern times.

But repentance is a pretty neat piece of vocabulary. It means to turn around and go in a new direction. To turn from our way to God's. To put the brakes on bad behavior in order to head back to the Lord.

Repentance is first and foremost for unbelievers. They are heading away from God and he calls them back to himself. It is the message of the gospel and the indicator of true faith in Christ.

But repentance is for believers also. In many little ways we all follow paths that lead us away from God rather than toward him. It can be a grudge that we are holding, refusing to let go as it creates bitterness and hatred in our hearts. It can be a secret sin, hidden from others—some activity that would shame the name of Christ. Perhaps it is something we are *not* doing—a message of hope we are not sharing, a relationship we are not working on, time or resources that we won't share with those in need.

Today's lesson focuses on Jonah's repentance. Your students will learn that the way of the Christian life is to turn toward Christ each and every day. We check our course. We look away from the distractions and diversions. Moment-by-moment repentance keeps us from straying and makes us useful in God's kingdom.

WAXING UP

♛ THE MIRROR AND THE MAZE

Materials needed:
Five copies of the reproducible maze on page 37 of this book; masking tape; writing utensils; five hand mirrors; a reward such as a snack or book of mazes for the game winner

Make five copies of the "Mirror Maze" student sheet found at the end of this lesson plan. Tape them to the wall so that five volunteers can have a race by attempting to solve the maze.

As your group is arriving, recruit five volunteers. As you begin class, give each volunteer a pencil and a mirror. Stand them by the mazes and say, **"You cannot look directly at the maze. Instead you must face away from it, look at the maze through the mirror and reach your arm back to draw. If you find yourself going in the wrong direction, stop and correct your path. Ready, set, go!"**

Because the image is reversed in the mirror, most kids will struggle to go the way they want and will find themselves correcting their path often. Give a prize to the winner.

Conclude this activity by saying something like this: **"You have seen how difficult it was for the contestants to go in the direction they wanted to go. The Christian life is sometimes like this. Today we are going to talk about what happens when we get to the place where we realize we need to correct our path."**

Continue with your next chosen activity.

♛ ♛ CHANGING DIRECTIONS

Materials needed:
Street map of your community; marker

To begin this activity, display a street map of your community on which you've marked the location of your church with a large dot. Have a student come forward and mark where he or she lives.

Tell students to shout out the directions one would need to follow in order to drive from the church to the person's house. They may say something like: "Drive west on that big street there and then go two blocks up." Whatever they say, use your marker to go in the exact opposite direction.

When the students point out your error, ask, **"What must I do to get there?"** The answer you are looking for is: *"Turn around and go back."*

Explain that today's session deals with the word "repent," which means to "turn around and go back."

Conclude by saying, **"Today, we'll look at God's desire that we all stop going our own way, and that we need to turn around and go *his* way."**

◆2 TAKING OFF

♕ FISHBONE SERENADE

Tell your students to work in pairs on the "Fishbone Serenade" section of the reproducible student sheet on page 39 of this book. Have them share with the whole group the tunes they have written . . . and sing them if they dare!

♕ ♕ THE OLFACTORY JONAH

Before class, go to the market and get a nice smelly fish. Locate a room that is much too small for your group and which can be darkened completely. Put the fish somewhere in the room so that the odor permeates the place. Grab a penlight and a Bible, and you are ready for a reading of the second chapter of Jonah that your students will never forget.

When ready to begin, take your students to the doorway of the room you will use. Before you enter, tell them, **"Today we are going to attempt to duplicate some of the conditions that helped Jonah come to a place where he was ready to turn around and go God's way. The experience may not be pleasant, but then the penalty phase of sin rarely is."**

Cram everybody in, turn on your penlight and shut the door. Be prepared for a lot of complaining about the smelly, hot and cramped conditions. When you come to the last verse of Jonah chapter 2 (where the fish barfs out Jonah), open the door and let your group out.

Go back to your regular meeting place and finish the story by reading chapter 3 of Jonah.

Involve your students in discussion by asking the following questions:

• **When do you think Jonah's repentance was genuine—while he was in the fish or after he was barfed out? Why?**

• **What is the significance of sackcloth and ashes?** (It is the oriental way to show great sorrow.)

• **Why do you think the people of Nineveh were told to dress their animals in sackcloth and ashes?** (Probably to show that they were super, super sorry.)

• **What would be the modern equivalent of sackcloth and ashes?**

• **Do you think the message of repentance is popular today? Why or why not?**

• **Do you see repentance as a onetime thing or as a regular event? Why?**

Materials needed:
Reproducible student sheet on page 39 of this book; Bibles; writing utensils

Materials needed:
A fish from the market; a small room prepared as described in the text; a penlight; a Bible

Materials needed:
Reproducible student sheet on page 39 of this
book; Bibles; writing utensils

♕ ♕ ♕ **TURNAROUND TOWN**

Tell everyone to read the third chapter of Jonah. Have them work individually to complete "Turnaround Town" on the student sheet. Then ask students to share with the group what they have circled or squared and why.

3 FULLY BARRELED

Materials needed:
Reproducible student sheet on page 39 of this
book; writing utensils

♕ **A PERSONAL REPENTANCE**

Ask your students to take a look at the "Personal Repentance" section of the student sheet. They are to prayerfully consider if there are any areas of their lives that need to be turned around. Allow time for them to fill in the arrows with those areas that need to be addressed. Encourage them to be specific in writing what they plan to do *starting today!*

Materials needed:
A place to hold a prayer meeting

♕ ♕ **PRAYING FOR REPENTANCE**

Individuals get going the wrong way—so do whole societies such as Nineveh. Organize a special prayer meeting for the specific purpose of praying that our society (town, city, state, country and world) might turn toward God. The prayer meeting doesn't have to be long to be effective. If you want, you can have your students write out their prayers in advance.

* **One Final Note: Don't forget to get rid of that smelly fish!**

Check This . . .
Play the song "Father Thy Will Be Done," by Carolyn Arends, from her Feel Free release. Use it at the end of the session as a time of meditation.

MIRROR MAZE

DO NOT TOUCH THE WALLS!

This maze looks pretty simple. But, what happens when you have to complete it while looking into a mirror? You cannot look directly at the maze—you must face away from it, look into the maze through the mirror and reach your arm back to draw. If you find yourself going in the wrong direction, stop and correct your path. Ready, set, go!

FISHBONE SERENADE

Read the second chapter of Jonah. Notice the poetry that Jonah composed while being digested in the belly of the big guppy. Take his words, ideas or basic theme and redo these verses in the form of a short song or commercial jingle. You can use a famous tune or make up your own.

Turnaround Town

Read the third chapter of Jonah. Put a square around any words below that would be true of Jonah. Circle any words that would be true of Nineveh.

arrogant	teachable	afraid	smelly	happy	joyful	hungry	hardworking
penitent	mournful	dynamic	obedient	hostile	amused	thirsty	comforted
terrified	forgiven	repentant	itchy	tired	loud	bold	hardhearted
	confused		confident		sorry		obstinate

Think of someone you know who is heading off in the wrong spiritual direction.
What are some ways you would know if that person had truly turned toward God?

A Personal Repentance

When we take a hard look at ourselves, we sometimes find areas in which we are going in the opposite direction from that which God would have us go. Take a minute and consider your own life. Are there changes that need to be made?

In the top arrow, write one area of your life that needs to be turned around. In the second arrow, write what you will do to turn back to God starting today!

Every Christian has the same command as Jonah: Go into a hostile world to let people know about Christ.

We've been called to be evangelists—to share our faith in Christ. When we tell others about the way of salvation, we want it to be genuine, meaningful and done in a way that is most likely to be effective.

This session is designed to help your students be a part of a real evangelistic event. If done correctly, your students will be able to present the gospel to a number of their friends.

A BEACH PARTY

The theme for this event is a beach party. This can be done in the summer at a lake, pool or ocean. For even more fun, it can be done indoors during the dead of winter with snow on the ground.

◆1 THE SIZE

A fun beach party can be held on any scale—large or small. For some churches, a beach party may draw hundreds of kids. For a church with a small youth group, it may not be realistic to expect mobs of kids. As far as numbers go, if your own group is behind the outreach event, you can predict that there will be at least one new visitor for each involved church kid.

◆2 ENVIRONMENT

Make the environment as "beachy" as possible, especially if you are doing the party indoors. See if you can find some surfboards, water skis, beach towels, inflatable rafts, beach balls and the like. A lifeguard chair would

BEACH REACH

Event Text
Matthew 28:18-20

Focus
This is a special event—a beach party designed to bring young people into contact with Christ. It can be done either in the summer or in the dead of winter.

Goals
As a result of participating in this event, students will:

• Invite non-Christian friends to a beach party where they can hear about Christ.

• Be involved in planning, fundraising and other details.

• Receive training in effectively sharing the good news about Jesus.

Materials needed:
Surfboards; water skis; beach towels; inflatable rafts; beach balls; beach chairs; sand; palm trees; Hawaiian shirts; sunglasses; posters of tropical places; surf videos; VCR and monitor; volleyball net and ball; cold drinks

be a nice touch.

You may want to haul in some sand for your beach and some palms in pots to put around the place. Wear Hawaiian shirts, shorts and sunglasses.

Get your hands on some water sports magazines. Travel posters of tropical places can be mooched off travel agents to add to the feel of summer. Find some surf videos and project them on a big screen, dig up some surf tunes and blast them in the background. Don't forget the volleyball net and ice cold beverages.

3 Music

Materials needed:
Live band or CDs and CD player; sound system

If you can afford it, book a live Christian band to come and play for your kids. If you are trying to get a big-name band you may have budget shock, but there are plenty of less expensive "up and coming" music groups that would appeal to your kids. Remember that the band is not the main draw for this event, but merely part of the excitement.

Let your music group know the party's purpose. Discuss with them how they can be involved in making sure solid evangelism is taking place. The most useful bands are those that talk about Jesus both on the stage and after-ward one-on-one. In other words, they "walk their talk."

If a band is out of the question, how about a Christian DJ spinning some tunes? Spend a little bit of money to get a decent sound system. To teenagers, sound is every-thing!

4 Games

Materials needed:
Volleyball net and ball; water balloons; plastic tarps; surfboard or ironing board

You can rig up all kinds of games and stunts that will keep kids interested. Try some of these:
- VOLLEYBALL
- INDOOR WATER BALLOON TOSS (BREAK OUT THE PLASTIC TARPS)
- BALANCING ON A SURFBOARD (OR OLD IRONING BOARD) ATTACHED TO A PIVOT POINT

5 Try a Barbecue

Materials needed:
Food items; grill; chefs

Since kids love to eat, a BarBQ could be a central part of the party. Put some of your kids' parents in charge of this, or ask for some volunteer youth workers who really know how to cook. What about a couple of senior saints who aren't typically involved with teens? Throw a couple of leis on them, and away you go!

Make sure to use beach dinnerware.

◆ THE GOSPEL

Be very strategic about sharing the gospel in the midst of a beach party. You may want to consider not going with the typical thirty-minute message format. Try some of these:

- Printed materials
- Kids sharing briefly what Christ means to them
- A cool video presentation to get the message across
- Hand out a portion of the Bible. Navpress publishes an inexpensive but easy to read selection of the Bible called *The Message of Hope.*

Materials needed:
Printed or video materials that will help present the gospel

◆ MONEY

An event like this can drain a youth budget quickly. Make your kids part of the planning and fundraising efforts. Working to raise money will give your group a real sense of ownership of this outreach event. You can bet they will be talking the event up more if they have put in an investment. A modest cover charge at the door can also help to cut your costs, although it would be better to be able to give the event as a "gift" to your visitors.

Materials needed:
Gifts from those who have a heart for outreach

◆ PUBLICITY

Your students are the best publicity you have. Be sure your group is sold on the event and excited about bringing their non-Christian friends. They each have a "web of influence"—those within their sphere of friends and work associates who know them and trust them. Arm them with lots of flyers to hand out at school. Teach them that these flyers are simply a tool to help them do what they should be doing naturally—sharing their faith in Jesus! Start advertising well in advance so that kids can clear their schedules for the party.

Using colored paper, make photocopies of the promotional flyer on page 45 to help with your publicity efforts.

Materials needed:
Reproducible publicity flyer on page 45 of this book

◆ TIMING

Your beach party can serve as a springboard to launch more outreach events. Publicize your next few activities at the party. That way the partygoers will sense that you want them to come back and be involved in your life and the life of your group. While you're in the planning stage, ask students to help you plan the next few activities that might help reach their friends.

◆10 FOLLOW UP

Don't forget to get names and addresses so that you can do a mailing for upcoming events, regular Bible studies and the like. Try to solicit information without using "Christianese," the language understood only by those who have been going to church for a long time. Encourage some of your computer-literate kids to create a database of those visitors who come to the event.

You may want to use a team of kids and adult workers to write personal notes or postcards to thank each newcomer who attends. Everyone loves to get mail, and teens are no exception.

Finally, pray that God will water the seeds of your efforts. Then, watch him work!

BEACH BLAST!

GRAB A FRIEND AND JOIN THE FUN

DATE _____

TIME _____

LOCATION _____

ITEMS TO BRING _____

OTHER EMPOWERED YOUTH PRODUCTS FROM STANDARD PUBLISHING

FOR GUYS ONLY
Young Men Behaving Godly

By Michael Kast

A four-session elective for junior-high and senior-high guys that will really get them thinking about what it takes to be a real man of God. A bonus event includes manly games and activities. Includes reproducible student sheets, numerous options and suggestions for using contemporary Christian music.
Order number 26-23307 (ISBN 0-7847-0737-5)

FOR GIRLS ONLY
Fearless and Female for God

By Jane Vogel

This four-session elective for junior-high and senior-high girls deals with God's plan for them to be both strong and gentle. A bonus girls-only sleepover is included as well as reproducible sheets, open-ended questions for in-depth discussion, flexible learning activities and contemporary music suggestions.
Order number 26-23308 (ISBN 0-7847-0738-3)

IT'S A SHEEP'S LIFE
Grazing in the 23rd Psalm
A creative study of Psalm 23

By Mike Nappa
Four sessions designed to help junior-high and senior-high teens entrust their lives to the loving Shepherd of their souls. Also includes a bonus event—a children's carnival put on by your teens. Two reproducible student sheets per lesson, contemporary Christian music suggestions and a boatload of options!
Order number 26-23305 (ISBN 0-7847-0735-9)

CLUELESS EVANGELISM:
How to Share Your Faith When You Haven't Got a Clue

By Michael Kast

A four-session elective for junior-high students (plus a bonus session that is an outreach event). The "kids reaching kids" strategy really works without coercing students to share their faith. Includes reproducible student sheets, numerous options and suggestions for using contemporary Christian music.
Order number 26-23302 (ISBN 0-7847-0612-3)

TO ORDER, CONTACT YOUR LOCAL CHRISTIAN BOOKSTORE.
(IF THE BOOK IS OUT OF STOCK, YOU CAN ORDER BY CALLING 1-800-543-1353.)